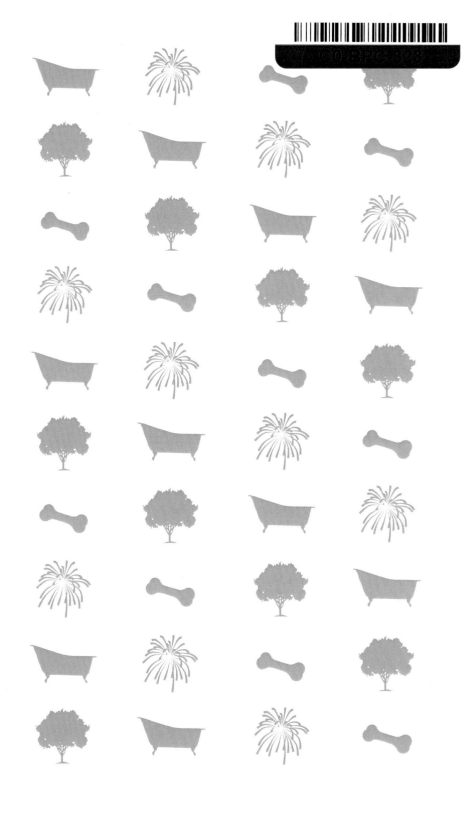

Piper's First Experiences

Mariah Leal

ISBN 978-0-9911246-0-2

❧ DEDICATION ☙

First of all to "Piper" who gave me a way to continue to work with my knowledge of dogs even with my disabilities. She has inspired me so much that now one book has turned into a series of five books.

To Robert, my love, my supporter, my rock; thank you for everything!

And a special thank you to our dear friends Gerry and Marie.

❦ CONTENTS ❧

❧ INTRODUCTION ❧

Here I am, Piper, back again with a whole new set of adventures to share with you! Guess what? I had a Birthday. I am now five months old. I can't believe I have been in my new home for almost three months now! For a puppy, five months old is a lot older than it is for children. Puppies grow very quickly and do more grown-up things at an early age compared to children.

I have lost all my baby teeth now and I have almost all my adult teeth. You won't have all of your adult teeth until you are about 12 years old. Mom is working with me on my training. I am very good at sit and sit/stay. That is where mom makes me sit, tells me to stay and walks away from me. I can also do this when I am lying down. I can't move until mom says "Piper, Come!" Then I get up, trot over to mom and sit in front of her and that's when I get a treat. It's a lot of fun and mom mixes up the order of the commands. Sometimes she walks around me instead of just away from me. She wants to make sure that I respond the right way to all my commands no matter what the situation is.

I learned a lot of new things since I talked to you last. I hope you enjoy reading all about my new adventures! The world is so big and there are so many new things to learn about and experience. Even if things seem a little hard at first, you will find if you keep trying, you can do it! I'm excited to tell you what I've been doing so let's start reading chapter one!

❧ CHAPTER 1 ❧
My Family Tree

Today mom did something very different with me. She took me outside and dad came with us. Mom told me to stand. I didn't know that command. Of course, I know how to stand; I do that naturally, so I couldn't understand why mom was telling me to do that. Well as mom explained it all my relatives are very important in the dog world. My parents, grandparents, and great-grandparents are almost all Champions. Mom has a piece of paper that shows my relatives and it is called my pedigree. People have one too. Theirs is called a Family Tree. It shows your parents, grandparents and even your aunts, uncles, and cousins. So when mom bought me she also got a copy of my pedigree. You can go back as far as you want and see all of your relatives. You should see if your parents have a copy of your family tree. If not, it may make a nice project to work on together as a family.

Well, getting back to my pedigree, all but three of my relatives are Champions. That means that they are very close to looking and acting like the perfect Bullmastiff. If someone wants their dog to have a litter of pups, they should look at the pedigrees to get a good match between the mother and the father dog. You become a Champion by going to dog shows and competing against other dogs of your breed. The judge watches how you run around the ring and then he examines you. He feels your muscles, looks at your teeth, and how you stand. You have to stand very still but show that you have a good expression. That means you should look like you are alert and interested in being in the show and that you want to win. Mom and my breeder don't really have plans for me to enter these types of shows. However, mom says it never hurts to learn these things especially when you are young. While mom was stacking me (making me stand still like they do at the shows), dad was taking some pictures so we could see what I looked liked. Mom could also see how I am developing. As I am growing, mom and dad can take more pictures to see what changes there are in me. Then mom can decide if these types of shows (they are called conformation shows) will be good for me to enter. Here is a picture of my doggie mom, Maddy. She is already a Champion. Isn't she pretty? Mom says that whether you're a show dog or not you need to always look your best. You need to be clean, have your nails clipped, and be brushed.

CHAPTER 2

My Extended Family

In my first book, I told you about my new family that I live with now in New York. R.J. and Maiya, are my new mom and dad, and all my animal brothers and sisters. Well I also have extended family. That means other family members like aunts and uncles, cousins, grandparents, and sometimes close friends that are like family. You may even call them aunt and uncle.

Mom and dad have two very close friends that are like family. Their names are Kathy and Nick. They have three

children. Since mom and dad are very close to them, mom and dad are like an aunt and uncle to the children. And my grandma (Maiyas' mom) is like their grandma. This is Nicky. He is eight years old and he is a very smart boy.

He was best friends with mom and dad's other dog, Dakota, who was a Great Dane. Nicky and Dakota grew up together. I hope I can be Nicky's' best friend too, like Dakota was!

Mom knew Nicky since he was born and she used to help out taking care of him. Then Nicky's mom was going to

have another baby and boy did they get a surprise! Kathy had two babies at the same time, so they are twins. Now Nick and Kathy have three children. The twins are girls. Their names are Apollina and Mila. They are five years old and they are very pretty. I got to go to their birthday party when they turned 4 years old.

Mila likes to stand on her head, balance on things, and do a split. She would be very good at gymnastics because those are things you have to know how to do.

Apollina likes to dance and sing. She likes to climb too. When mom goes over to visit, she loves to brush moms' long hair.

I really am enjoying getting to know them and I want to be best friends with all three of them. I already really like their mom and dad. And I am especially glad that they are part of my extended family!

❧ CHAPTER 3 ❧
The Bath

I had fun the other night with mom, but little did I know that she was preparing me for quite an experience of my own. It was late and mom had taken me out for my last potty of the night. Daddy was still out with Zaniah so, mom took me into the bathroom with her. She told me she was going to take a shower. She said, "You stay with mommy Piper". I had been in the bathroom before but, not for very long. Well, mom got into something that looked like a big rectangular bowl. She called it the tub. I was wondering what was going to happen next. Then I heard water running so I peeked around the curtain. Mom said to me "See the water, Piper?" She put some in her hand and let me sniff it. Then I knew what it was and I started to lick it. Then mom said "I'm going to put the shower on". Now the water was coming from up above mom instead of out of the faucet. I moved away from the curtain and mom called me back. She showed me that the water was running on her as I poked my head around the curtain. I tried sniffing and mom took the shower down and brought it over to me. She showed me the water running in her hand. I started to lick the water and lick moms' knee. I didn't even realize that my head was getting a little wet. Then mom closed the curtain again because she didn't want me to get any soap in my mouth or my eyes. When she was all rinsed off she showed me the water again and now I had my front paws up on the rim of the tub. This was fun! My head and neck were a little wet so mom dried me off and put me to bed.

Mom was up early the next morning. She took me out-side for my potty time and then fed me. She took me out again and put me back in my crate. Then she said "Mommy will see you in a little while" and I know when she says this, it means she will be back soon. Mom and dad left. Sometime later daddy came home to get me and we went in the car. I love going for car rides because mom and dad have taken me in the car a lot since they brought me home. Well, daddy brought me to grandmas' house and boy was I surprised to see that mom was there. I was so excited! I went outside and ran around in grandmas' backyard. It's fun there because grandma has a fence and I don't have to be on a leash. At home I have to be on my leash because we don't have a fence and mom says I can get hurt. There could be other dogs running loose or I could run into the street where there are cars and I could get hurt. So at grandmas' I have a lot of fun being free to run as fast as I want! After I had some good play time mom said to me "You're going to get a bath Piper; whether you are a show dog or not you have to get used to having a bath". I had never had a bath so I wasn't sure what to expect. But somehow the words sounded a bit familiar. My mom was a professional dog groomer. She would take care of other peoples' dogs by brushing them, giving them baths, cleaning their ears, and clipping their nails. Sometimes when a dog has long hair and their owners don't brush them, their hair gets all knotted up and it hurts them. Mom would spend a long time trying to get the knots out of their hair. Sometimes they are so badly knotted that mom has to give them a haircut. So mom took me down to her grooming shop. She wasn't sure how I would do on the stairs, because there are a lot of stairs. At home we only have a few stairs. I was a little afraid to go down but once I started I was fine. I even went faster as I got near the bottom.

Remember I told you dogs get to know about things by sniffing? Well there were so many smells from all the different dogs that had been in the grooming shop, the smell of cleaners, and shampoo. My little wrinkly nose was going faster than I think it ever went before. Well, the only other time I remember it going that fast was when I went to the Veterinarians' office. That's the animal doctor. I looked around the shop and daddy brought some folding steps to put up against the tub. This tub is on legs and is much taller than our tub at home. Then mom said "Okay Piper, time for your bath". She took my leash and led me to the steps that went up to the tub. I wasn't sure if I wanted to go up the three steps because the steps felt funny. They were plastic coated and had holes in them. Once mom and dad helped me on to the steps I ran right up to the third step. Then I had to step down into the tub. I wasn't sure I wanted a bath at this point but mom coaxed me in and I just jumped in without looking back. I have to say once mom showed me the water I remembered that it was kind of fun when mom took her shower. So I decided to give it a try. Mom was very gentle and her friend, Darlene was there helping to hold me. Daddy took a couple of pictures of me.

The first picture dad took he forgot to turn the cell phone around and he took a funny picture of himself, hehe. The shampoo smelled nice. It was a little cold when mom first put it on me. When mom started to rub the shampoo into my coat it felt like a massage. Kind of like someone is scratching your back and massaging your muscles with their fingers all at once. I really liked that part. Then mom rinsed all the soap off of me. Mom was telling Darlene how important it is to get all the shampoo off of your dog.

Mom had to make sure she rinsed under my armpits, my tummy and all the little creases to make sure all the soap was out. Mom said if any soap stayed on my skin I could get an irritation. That means my skin would get red and itchy. After I was rinsed off they wrapped me in a towel and put me on the grooming table to be dried.

The table was nice, it had a rubber top. It didn't feel like the steps did. It was comfy sitting up there on the table with the towel around me but, I still wanted to investigate the whole grooming shop! Mom cleaned my ears with little cotton pads and some ear cleaner. There was no brown stuff on the pads which meant I had nice clean ears. Then thcy put a leash on me that mom tied to a pole on the table. This keeps wiggly puppies and dogs from jumping off the table. Then daddy brought over a big machine with a long hose on it. I wasn't sure I wanted to see what that was all about, it looked a little scary. I trusted mom so I decided to be brave. When dad turned it on a lot of air came out of it. I didn't really want this air blowing on my short fur. It felt like it was pushing my fur in the wrong direction. Then mom shut it off and let me smell the nozzle of the hose. It really didn't smell like anything except rubber and air. We tried it again and I let mom dry me a little more but then I started wiggling around on the table. So mom told dad to turn off the dryer. Mom wanted me to experience a little of everything that I will have to deal with when I am groomed, so next she put me in one of the cages. I am used to those because of my crate at home. She put down a comfy towel for me to lay on. Then mom brought a big machine that had tall legs over to my cage. She let me smell it through the bars and then she turned it on. It was another type of dryer. This one didn't blow so hard and it was warmer. They left me in the cage with the dryer on for about 10 minutes.

Really they were just on the other side of the base-ment, right behind the grooming shop area. I know mom would never leave me completely by myself especially going through something I wasn't used to doing. Then they took me out of the cage and put me back on the grooming table. Mom checked me all over and brushed me. Then she put my collar and leash back on and sprayed me with something that

smelled very nice. She put me down on the floor and it was time to go back upstairs. I was jumping around and going in circles because I felt so good after my first grooming. Mom and dad helped me up the stairs because these stairs had an opening at the back of the step. I wanted to stick my little head through to see what was over there but mom kept saying "Piper, keep your head up". After we got halfway up the stairs I wasn't even interested in seeing between the steps. I just wanted to get upstairs and show everyone how pretty I looked! Mom and dad helped me through my first grooming. They stayed with me and made sure I knew what everything was so I wouldn't be afraid. Just like your moms and dads would do for you. They went with you when you got a haircut, especially for the first time and they stay with you if you have to go to the doctor. That's because they love us. They want us to know these things are good for us even if we don't understand it at the time. Anyway, grandma told me how pretty I looked and gave me some treats. I just pranced around because I knew I looked pretty and I felt so good!

🎵 CHAPTER 4 🎵
We're Having Company

Something special is happening this weekend. Mom's friend from upstate New York is coming down for a visit. Mom said she is my Aunt Carol and mom got to know her because of Zaniah. That's the Akita that lives with us (my doggie sister).

Mom and Carol haven't seen each other in about two years so they are very excited about the visit. Aunt Carol has

a lot of Akitas and two small dogs that are part Pekingese and part Japanese Chin. The last time Carol came to visit she brought Isaiah with her. He is one of her Akitas. Mom said this time she is going to bring Isaiah and her two little dogs too! So, I get to have three dogs to meet and play with for the weekend! It's going to be so much fun! They will all stay here with us and then we are going to grandma's house and run around together in the backyard! Then mom said that Aunt Carol, Isaiah, me and mom will go to visit Aunt Darlene at her store on Saturday night. We will get to hang out outside and sit around the picnic table and meet all kinds of people. For a little puppy I sure have an exciting social life!

Mom and dad have been busy with their usual chores plus they are doing some extra straightening up for when Aunt Carol comes. We have to make room for Aunt Carol and Isaiah, plus room for the crate that the two little dogs will sleep in. Well mom and dad went to pick up Aunt Carol, Isaiah, Cana and Neko (they are two little dogs and they are nine months old). Isaiah sure is a big Akita and Cana and Neko are tiny. Aunt Carol was nice,

I could tell right away that she really loved dogs and was a good mom. They got to our house in the evening and Aunt Carol had crates to bring in for her puppies. She also had their food and toys, and her own suitcase to bring in. Dad helped set up everything and then mom and Aunt Carol talked a little and then the introductions started. I had to meet her dogs and mom said we have to do it slowly so that everyone would be calm. Zaniah already knew Isaiah but didn't know the two puppies. One by one, we all got to sniff each other.

Mom and Aunt Carol made sure we were on our leashes and watched us closely when we met. Mom says you can't just let two dogs that don't know each other be together unsupervised. We all got along well.

Mom taught me that it is important to share toys. She told me that the puppies are visiting and because they are guests in our home I have to play nice and share with them. I got to play with the Cana and Neko for awhile and then we all went to bed.

⟡ CHAPTER 5 ⟡
To Grandmother's House We Go!

We all got up the next morning and mom said we are going over to grandma's house. Oh, I was so excited! I love going to grandmas but now I was going with my new doggie friends. We all piled in the car and I had to ride in a crate. I hadn't been in a crate in the car since mom and dad picked me up at the airport. Actually it was the same crate I was in on the airplane. You know what? I have gotten a lot bigger since then. I had lots of room to stretch out when I was in the crate on the airplane but now I can't. I was glad it was a short ride because it was a little squishy in there. Now I know what mom means when she says "Piper you are getting so big"! Mom and Aunt Carol put us all in crates so that we would be safer in the car. It's like when you are small and have to sit and get strapped into the car seat. That is the safest place for little children to sit and crates are safe for puppies. Even Isaiah was in a crate and he is a big dog. I couldn't wait to get to grandmas and show my new puppy friends the big back yard. Isaiah and I went into the yard first with our moms. I felt like a big dog showing him the yard that I get to play in. He wasn't that interested in playing with me, he just wanted to sniff all around because he could smell grandmas' dogs. Besides he's a grown-up dog and didn't want to do the things I like to do in the yard. I like to run around and hide under the bushes so mom can't see me.

And I still try to pick up things in my mouth. Then mom has to come over and open my mouth and take out whatever I picked up. She said there are certain plants that can make me sick if I eat them. Sticks can be dangerous too. If I swallow a piece it could get stuck somewhere and then I would have to go see the veterinarian. If he can't see it he would have to take an x-ray. An x-ray is a picture of the inside of your body. This lets the doctor see something you swallowed so he knows where it is and if it will be a problem. It's very important that puppies don't eat sticks, stones, or plants. Since puppies don't have hands like you do, we investigate things with our mouth and sometimes that can get us into trouble.

After Isaiah and I had some time outside, then Cana and Neko got to come out in the yard. Even though they are older than me, they are small so I had to be careful not to play too rough with them. Then we all went inside and grandma brought her dog Remy out to see us. Remy is 12 years old and she is like a doggie grandma. She is very gentle with puppies and she teaches older dogs to mind their manners.

Grandmas other dog Tehya, didn't come out to see us because she can be a little wild. She runs around and knocks things over and chases the cats. Remy keeps her in line but with so many pups in the house grandma said it was better that Tehya stayed behind the gate in the other room. We did get to say hi to Tehya through the gate. Remy and Isaiah said hello, they sniffed each other all over and then Remy spent most of her time watching over Cana and Neko. She nuzzled them with her nose and gently put her paw on them almost like she was petting them. We all had fun and of course grandma gave us all some treats! Grandmas are good for giving treats. They spoil us a little and sometimes mom has to tell grandma "Piper has had enough treats for today". Then mom, Carol, and Grandma spent time talking and eating lunch. People spend a lot of time talking. We all took a nap while the people were visiting. We all got to have a little more playtime outside before it was time to leave. When we saw the leashes come out we knew it was time to go. We all got back into our crates in the van and came back home.

❦ CHAPTER 6 ❦
Our Friends are Going Home

I knew it was getting close to the time when Aunt Carol and my doggie friends were going to have to leave for home. Mom and Aunt Carol were taking pictures with all of us and daddy too.

Then they took Zaniah and Isaiah outside for some pictures. They are both beautiful Akitas!

They finished the pictures and Aunt Carol started putting her bags and the crates in the car. I could tell mom wasn't so happy anymore. We sat on the couch for a little bit and Aunt Carol cuddled me. I was lying on my back resting my

head on her tummy. Mom hugged Isaiah, Cana, and Neko. Then they took us for a walk so we could all go potty. When we came back in mom hugged Aunt Carol and I noticed mom had watery eyes. I wasn't sure what that meant but it did make mom look sad. Mom put me in my crate and said "mommy will be right back". So, I lied down in my crate for a nap because I was tired from the big day. Then I heard the door close and then everything was quiet. I really wasn't sure what good-bye meant and why mom seemed a little sad. Soon I heard the front door open and I got all excited. Mom came right in the bedroom and let me out of my crate and I came bounding into the living room. I was all excited to see mom and dad but when I looked around nobody else was with them. The crates were gone from the living room and there was no sign of Aunt Carol and my new doggie friends. I finally figured out that good-bye meant they weren't coming back here and I guess that's why mom looked sad. But mom told me that they would come back to visit again and maybe one day we would go to Aunt Carols' house. Her house is far away and that is why they don't get to see each other as much as they would like. But we had a fun weekend and I can't wait to see them again!

❦ CHAPTER 7 ❧
Pipers' First Thunderstorm

Wow! Do I have a story to tell! I have never seen anything like this before in my life! It all started on a Saturday when I noticed mom and dad were not acting the way they usually do. They were acting very serious. Dogs are very good at sensing things. We can tell a lot about peoples' moods by watching their body language. Since dogs can't talk, when we meet a strange dog we watch their body language. That is how we know if they are friendly or not. We can tell if they are calm, or ready for a fight.

I will tell you more about reading a dogs' body language in another book. Now back to my story. So I watched mom and dads' body language. They seemed a little tense. Mom went around getting some little lanterns and checking them to see if they made light. Mom also got some candles and made sure they were in glass holders. Dad went outside and tied up the garbage cans. Mom said "Piper, we're going to have a storm!", but she said it with a happy tone.

Well when the storm started there was a lot of wind, rain, and flashes of light outside. I was listening to all the sounds because as you know all dogs have good hearing. I heard things blowing around outside and the rain on the roof and against the windows. But then I heard something that made me jump! It was a loud crashing noise. Mom knew I was upset and she asked me "Do you hear the thunder, Piper? That's just part of the storm". Then instead of petting me when the thunder came, mom started to play with me. We played with my stuffed toys and my ball. Then mom made me do my sit and stay exercises and I got treats. And you know what? Before I knew it, the thunderstorm was over and I wasn't even scared. The next time we had a storm like that I knew it was going to be okay and that it was just a storm and it would be over soon. That's because mom helped me through the first storm and taught me not to be afraid.

This is why mom says it's so important for puppies to experience as much as they can while they're little, so they won't be afraid of strange things when they grow up.

❧ CHAPTER 8 ❧
The Fourth of July

Today was the first time I experienced the holiday of the Fourth of July, Independence Day. I wasn't sure what it was all about. Mom put out the American flag this morning. Then I heard mom and dad talking about this being the celebration of our country's' birthday. They were talking about barbeques, parties, and something called fireworks.

The day started out with mom spending time with me; that was fun. Then I saw mom getting her things together. But then mom said "Piper, nappy nappy time, in your crate" and I knew I wasn't going with them. Mom and dad left and they were gone for awhile. I took a nap, then chewed on my bone and played with my stuffed toy. After that I got sleepy again and took another nap. Before I knew it mom and dad came home. I was so excited to see them. I was jumping around and giving them kisses. They were at a barbeque and they would have taken me with them except it was hot today. Mom is always very careful about not taking me out in the car when the temperature outside is very warm. Puppy's bodies work differently than people and they cannot cool down as quickly. So that is why I stayed home with Zaniah in the nice air conditioned house.

When it started to get dark outside I heard some noises in the distance. My ears went up and I looked towards the window and I heard it again. It went bang, bang bang. I wasn't sure if I liked this and I know mom could tell I was unsure about the noises. She said "That's fireworks, Piper. Listen to the nice

fireworks". But I didn't think they were very nice and my ears went back against my head and I had a funny look on my face. So mom put some music on and she was singing. She got one of my toys and played with me. She was trying to distract me from the noise of the fireworks so I wouldn't be afraid. Then the bangs got louder and closer together. I went to go behind mom's legs to hide because I was a little scared. Mom wouldn't let me hide though. She got up and started singing again and moving around funny (I think it was dancing) and clapping her hands.

Then daddy came in and started to play with me. I kind of forgot about the noise of the fireworks for awhile. Mom kept the music on, gave me my crackly toy and went back to the computer. Then all of a sudden the fireworks got very loud and very fast. Mom got up and got a few of my treats and made me do some of my commands. I did my sit and stay and mom gave me my treats. Then it stopped! No more fireworks! We just heard a few little ones after that. When mom took me for my last potty and my walk I could hear a few fireworks in the background but I wasn't really scared. I still wanted to walk with mom. So, we walked and met Zaniah and dad, and then we came home. So, I guess my first Fourth of July wasn't too bad.

☜ CHAPTER 9 ☞
More Firsts for Piper

I had some more things that I experienced for the first time. One of them was riding in an elevator. Mom had a doctors' appointment and dad took her and I came along. I couldn't go into the office but mom said she wanted me to get used to everything so off we went into the elevator.

First we had to go down in the elevator. It felt funny at first that we were moving but my feet were standing still. My tummy felt like it dropped a little but I was okay. Then the doors opened and we were on the first floor. We got out and walked a little and then went back into the elevator and went back up to the third floor again. Mom and dad both said I did very well in the elevator. Mom went to her appointment and dad took me to the car. But I got a little confused going out of the door. They had big windows on each side of the door. Dad wasn't watching me even though I had my collar and leash on and I walked into the window instead of the door. It didn't hurt but I sat back and looked for a minute like who moved the door? Dad had a smile on his face. I know if mom saw that she would have said to dad "you have to watch Piper, she's still a baby". Dad and I went in the car and waited for mom.

My next first experience was going to a birthday party! It was at our neighbors' house.

I thought we were just going for a potty walk but then mom took me to the neighbors. We came around the corner and I saw a bunch of people sitting around a table. I knew two of them, but the others were new to me. They all liked me and I couldn't wait to say hello. My tail was wagging back and forth and I just wanted to jump on everyone. Mom told me "no jump" and "sit". It was so hard because I was so excited to find out who all these people were. Then a young woman I met before came out of the house and I was very excited because she has a little girl that is not quite two years old. Her name is Emily. Mom kept saying "that's the baby Piper, easy with the baby". Somehow I sensed that she was a baby too because I smelled her and tried not to jump on her. I licked her feet and she giggled and I even nuzzled her tummy. She giggled even more and that made me want to get more excited. They put Emily down and mom made me sit and we were all pretty calm. But then Emily wanted to play with me and she was squealing and moving her arms all around and that really got me excited. I jumped up and put my paws in the air. Mom told me "no!" and made me sit again. It was really hard for me to be calm with Emily running and squealing. But mom was determined that I was going to learn to control myself. She told Emily's mom that when Emily runs and makes squealing noises it gets me too excited. After a bit we all calmed down and I was tired from wanting to play. I learned the lesson that I have to be calmer with little children. Emily is starting to learn that she needs to be calm around dogs because they get excited and could knock her down and accidentally hurt her. It is just as important for children to know how to act around dogs as it is for dogs to learn how to act around children. You should never walk up to a dog you don't know. When you are with your parents and you see a dog being walked always ask the owner if you can pet the dog. Whenever new people are around or there is a new situation mom takes advantage of it to socialize me more. Today when we were on our potty walk the mailman was coming with our mail. Mom really wasn't sure if he wanted to meet me, but I was very curious about him. So, when he came around the front of the yard the mailman asked mom if I was friendly. Mom said yes and we walked over to him and he bent down to pet me. He had a big bag on his shoulder and a bunch of papers and magazines in his hands and a funny hat on. When he first bent down to pet me I felt like I wanted to run away but, mom wouldn't let me go far and coaxed me back to say hello. Well, once I got a little sniff of him I could tell this mailman liked dogs. He was petting me and I was wiggling around and I jumped up on him and he scratched behind my ears. That felt so good, puppies like being scratched behind their ears. Now I learned that the mailman is on our property to bring us the mail and I don't have to bark at him. Sometimes I even bring the mail in for mom.

Later on, in the evening when it was still light outside, mom took me out. I wanted mom to walk me on the sidewalk and she let me because it was cooler then it was during the day. Mom won't let me walk on the sidewalk in the middle of the day in this hot summer weather. The sidewalks get very hot and mom says that I can burn my pads on the bottom of my feet. You know when you go outside barefoot and the sidewalk burns your feet, well that's how it feels on my little paw pads. Children can put on sandals or sneakers to protect their feet. So there mom and I were feeling the evening breeze and she let me walk with her on the sidewalk. She was going to take me to the right. I kept hearing children playing at the other end of the street. Mom figured I wanted to investigate. Mom wasn't sure if I would go all the way

up to meet the children. I was determined to find out what they were doing up there and why they were making all the noise. The noise wasn't scary but it was a little loud. Mom kept coaxing me by saying "Piper, see the children playing? Do you want to go say hello to the children?" The closer we got the more excited I was getting. When we got near the children one boy was the first to come over. He asked mom "Does your dog bite"? Mom answered "No, she doesn't but don't run at her, just come to her calmly". See mom always looks out for me and children. The boy came over and I knew right away that he liked dogs. He knew just how to come up to me and before you knew it, I was giving him my paw and jumping up (mom didn't like that part) but the boy didn't seem to mind. Then the boys friends came over and I got to say hello to eight children! Wow! Eight at one time, that was fun. I wish we had been some place safe like grandmas' backyard so I could have run around with them without my leash! We had fun and mom thanked the children for coming and saying hello to me. Then mom and I started back home.

❧ CHAPTER 10 ☙
Practice, Practice, Practice

Of course, mom is making me practice the things I've learned. Now that I am teething (which means my adult teeth are coming in) I sometimes get distracted more easily. That happens to all puppies at this age. Our mouths are sore and sometimes we don't want to do our homework. Mom says it is very important that we continue not only practicing what we already know but learning new things as well. But on days that I don't feel well mom takes it easy with me. The more we learn when we're young the fewer problems we will have as adults. We want to be good canine members of society. The only way that can happen is with responsible doggie moms and dads that take the time to give us the proper training and socializing that we need.

I am really starting to know why mom is so consistent with my training and socializing. After hearing mom tell Aunt Darlene about how important it is to groom your dog and how if you don't take care of their coats then can actually have pain, I see now why grooming is important. So I have to learn how to behave during a bath and get used to all the equipment. I also understand how important it is to be around as many different things and people as I can. I have to know how to behave in all situations. I think you are getting a better idea of this also from reading about all my first experiences. It doesn't matter if a puppy (or dog) comes from a shelter or a breeder, because teaching that puppy or dog is what makes them a pet that will live with you all of their lives. So many dogs wind up in the animal shelters because their moms and dads don't train them properly and then they become frustrated with the dog. My mom says that is one reason it is very crowded in the shelters. Then those puppies and dogs have to wait for the right person to come along and adopt them. Sometimes mom says that is hard because since they weren't trained properly they may have some bad behaviors. So the person that adopts them has to work harder sometimes to teach them how to behave properly. This doesn't mean they won't be good dogs. And just like mom researched my breed when she picked me, people who adopt from shelters need to ask questions too. This way they will get a dog that will fit into their family well. Since there isn't always a lot of information on shelter dogs, the shelters themselves have to test the dogs to find out more about them. Does the dog get aggressive when he is eating? This happens when a dog wasn't fed properly and when they are given food they are afraid someone will try to take it away from them so they try to protect their food. Does the dog get along well with children, smaller animals, and cats? This is where a good shelter tests these dogs so they can find a forever home. Breeders have to do these things too so their dogs can find a forever home like I did. Grandma's two dogs, Remy and Tehya were both shelter dogs and they turned out to be very good for Grandma. Boy, this has been a lot of learning for a little one like me! But it shows I am growing up too!

I wonder what things mom has planned for me next. I know I am going to be starting school soon. I wonder what that will be like. I know I will get to meet other puppies my age. I wonder what they will teach us. I am sure that school is not the only thing I will have to look forward to, because if I know my mom, there will be a lot more exciting things that she will have planned for me. I am so excited about school. So make sure you read my next book to find out about all my adventures at puppy kindergarten. See you soon!

Piper